Spelling
Practice

Exercises devised by Brenda Apsley
an experienced author and editor who specialises
in writing early learning books for children
Illustrated by John Haslam

Learning Rewards is a home-learning programme designed to help your child succeed at school with the National Curriculum. It has been extensively researched with parents and teachers.

This book, *Spelling Practice*, and its companion title, *Spelling Skills*, cover important aspects of the National Curriculum at Key Stage I.

Children should start with the *Skills* books (with younger children this is important) and progress to the *Practice* books.

The *Skills* book teaches basic skills and new concepts through structured and enjoyable activities. The *Practice* book reinforces and builds on these skills by the essential repetition of exercises.

You will need to work through each page with your child and talk about what is required. The star symbol at the top of the page details the particular skills covered by the exercise as they relate to the National Curriculum. The content is progressive, so explain the importance of starting from the front of the book.

The fold-out progress chart is a useful record of your child's performance. Always reward your child's work with encouragement and a gold star sticker.

When you come to the end of the book you will find a fun, wipe-clean learning game.

series editor: Nina Filipek
series designer: Paul Dronsfield
Copyright © 1996 World International Limited.
All rights reserved.
Published in Great Britain by
World International Limited, Deanway Technology Centre,
Wilmslow Road, Handforth, Cheshire SK9 3FB.
Printed in Italy.
ISBN 0 7498 2712 2

Spelling

First and last-letter sounds

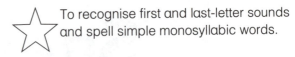

To recognise first and last-letter sounds and spell simple monosyllabic words.

Spell a word for each bee by writing in a missing letter.
The missing letters are at the **start** or **end** of the words.
There can be more than one right answer.

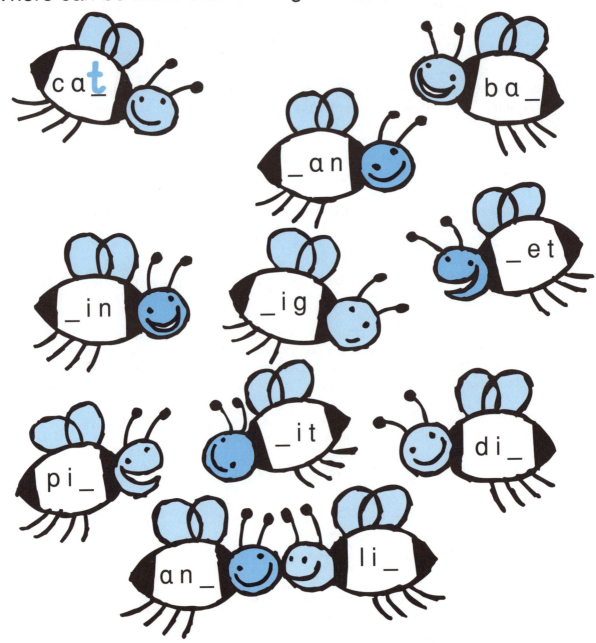

2

Spelling

First and last-letter sounds

_ u n

d o _

m a _

_ a t

_ o t

b u _

_ e d

c o _

_ u g

l o _

w e _

_ e n

m u _

3

Spelling

Words with a

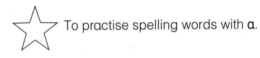 To practise spelling words with a.

Write **a** to spell the words. Spell each word three times.

h<u>a</u>t  <u>hat</u> <u>hat</u> <u>hat</u>

b _ t ___ ___ ___

l _ m p ____ ____ ____

f l _ g ____ ____ ____

h _ n d ____ ____ ____

_ p p l e _____ _____ _____

Tick the words that are spelled correctly. Spell them below.

cap ✓   van   bag   mat

cape   varn   bap   matt

___   ___   ___   ___

4

Spelling

 To practise spelling words with **e**.

Write **e** to spell the words. Spell each word three times.

b _ d  _ _ _   _ _ _   _ _ _

h _ n _ _ _   _ _ _   _ _ _

t _ n t  _ _ _ _   _ _ _ _   _ _ _ _

w _ b  _ _ _   _ _ _   _ _ _

p _ n  _ _ _   _ _ _   _ _ _

n _ s t  _ _ _ _   _ _ _ _   _ _ _ _

Tick the words that are spelled correctly. Spell them below.

pen   temt   beb   nest

penn   tent   bed   ness

_ _ _   _ _ _ _   _ _ _   _ _ _ _

Spelling

Words with **i**, **o** and **u**

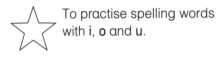

Write the letters **i**, **o** or **u** to spell the words.

Spell each word three times.

s _ n   _ _ _   _ _ _   _ _ _

c _ t   _ _ _   _ _ _   _ _ _

s _ c k   _ _ _ _   _ _ _ _   _ _ _ _

h _ l l   _ _ _ _   _ _ _ _   _ _ _ _

j _ g   _ _ _   _ _ _   _ _ _

t _ n   _ _ _   _ _ _   _ _ _

m _ g   _ _ _   _ _ _   _ _ _

d _ g   _ _ _   _ _ _   _ _ _

r a b b _ t   _ _ _ _ _ _   _ _ _ _ _ _   _ _ _ _ _ _

c a r r _ t    _ _ _ _ _ _   _ _ _ _ _ _   _ _ _ _ _ _

Spelling

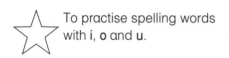 To practise spelling words with **i**, **o** and **u**.

Words with **i**, **o** and **u**

Rearrange the letters to spell the words correctly.
Spell each word twice more.

n u b   <u>bun</u>   _ _ _   _ _ _

g n i k   _ _ _ _   _ _ _ _   _ _ _ _

f x o   _ _ _   _ _ _   _ _ _

n u r   _ _ _   _ _ _   _ _ _

g o l   _ _ _   _ _ _   _ _ _

Spell the **i**, **o** or **u** words that finish the sentences.

The box is not small. It is <u>big</u>.   bug   bag   big

I can _ _ _ on one leg.   hip   hop   hold

I _ _ _ the ball with a bat.   hit   hat   hut

In summer the _ _ _ is _ _ _ .   hot   hat   sun

Words with **ck** and **st**

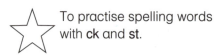

Choose **ck** or **st** to spell the words.
Spell the words to finish the sentences.

c h i _ _ A baby hen is called a _ _ _ _ _ _ .

_ _ a m p s Anna collects _ _ _ _ _ _ _ .

_ _ a r s The _ _ _ _ _ come out at night.

c l o _ _ Tick, tock, goes the _ _ _ _ _ _ .

l i _ _ Write a _ _ _ _ of things to do.

Tick the **ck** words that are spelled correctly.

| brock | ticket | lorck | sack | truck |
| brick | tikit | lock | seck | turck |

Tick the correct **st** words.

| stop | fast | larst | steck | first |
| stap | fest | last | stick | furst |

8

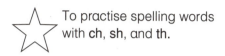

To practise spelling words with **ch**, **sh**, and **th**.

Words with **ch**, **sh**, **th**

Spell the words with **ch** and **sh** letters. Write each word twice, then cover the words. Can you spell the words on your own?

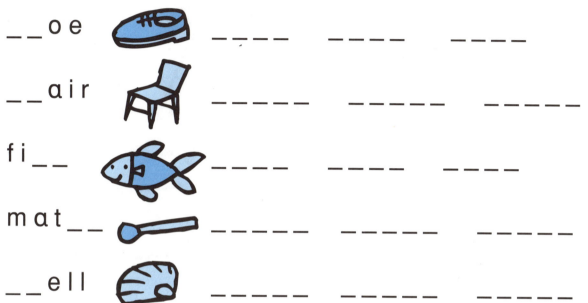

_ _ o e   _ _ _ _   _ _ _ _   _ _ _ _

_ _ a i r   _ _ _ _ _   _ _ _ _ _   _ _ _ _ _

f i _ _   _ _ _ _   _ _ _ _   _ _ _ _

m a t _ _   _ _ _ _ _   _ _ _ _ _   _ _ _ _ _

_ _ e l l   _ _ _ _ _   _ _ _ _ _   _ _ _ _ _

Underline all the words with **th** in the story below.

This is Joe Smith.

There are four people in the Smith family.

Joe has a brother called Tim.

Tim is older than Joe.

Tim and Joe live with their mother and father.

Words with 'magic e'

To practise spelling words with **a**, **i**, **o** and **u** with last letter **e**.

Add **e** to the picture words to spell new words.
Spell the **new** words.

can   + e = _ _ _ _

pin   + e = _ _ _ _

tap   + e = _ _ _ _

pan   + e = _ _ _ _

Spell each word twice, then cover and try to spell again, on your own this time. Draw lines to match the words and pictures.

nine   _ _ _ _   _ _ _ _   _ _ _ _

cube   _ _ _ _   _ _ _ _   _ _ _ _

rose   _ _ _ _   _ _ _ _   _ _ _ _

bone   _ _ _ _   _ _ _ _   _ _ _ _

line   _ _ _ _   _ _ _ _   _ _ _ _

Spelling

To practise spelling words with **a**, **i**, **o** and **u** with last letter **e**.

Words with 'magic e'

All the words in the crossword end with **e**.

Spell the words then complete the crossword.

I l _ k e = _ _ _ _

2 p o _ e = _ _ _ _

3 _ i t e = _ _ _ _

4 p _ g e = _ _ _ _

5 g _ t _ = _ _ _ _

6 t _ l e = _ _ _ _

7 m _ l e = _ _ _ _

8 m i _ e = _ _ _ _

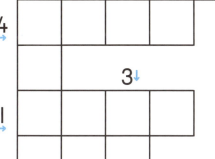

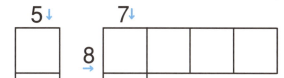

Words with **bl**, **cl**, **fl**, **gl**, **pl**, **sl**

To practise spelling words with letters bl, cl, fl, gl, pl and sl.

Write the letters that spell the words.

Write **bl**, **cl**, **fl**, **gl**, **pl** or **sl**. Spell each word three times.

_ _ i d e   _ _ _ _ _   _ _ _ _ _   _ _ _ _ _

_ _ a t e   _ _ _ _ _   _ _ _ _ _   _ _ _ _ _

_ _ o c k   _ _ _ _ _   _ _ _ _ _   _ _ _ _ _

_ _ a g   _ _ _ _   _ _ _ _   _ _ _ _

_ _ o b e    _ _ _ _ _   _ _ _ _ _   _ _ _ _ _

_ _ o w   _ _ _ _   _ _ _ _   _ _ _ _

Choose the right words from the list. Spell them.

The sky is _ _ _ _ .

We stick things with _ _ _ _ .

At night we go to _ _ _ _ _ .

Birds can _ _ _ .

I like to _ _ _ _ tag.

glue
fly
blue
play
sleep

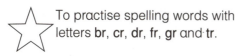

To practise spelling words with letters br, cr, dr, fr, gr and tr.

Words with **br**, **cr**, **dr**, **fr**, **gr**, **tr**

Write the letters **br**, **cr**, **dr**, **fr**, **gr**, or **tr** to spell each word.
Spell the words to finish the sentences.

_ _ u m   Baby bangs a _ _ _ _ .

_ _ o g   A _ _ _ _ can swim.

_ _ i c k   The wall needs one more _ _ _ _ _ _ .

_ _ i s p s   I like _ _ _ _ _ _ _ .

_ _ a s s   The _ _ _ _ _ is green.

_ _ a i n   The _ _ _ _ _ is late.

Read each word. Cover it. Then spell it on your own.

brown _ _ _ _ _   tree _ _ _ _   crab _ _ _ _

drive _ _ _ _ _   draw _ _ _ _   cry _ _ _

front _ _ _ _ _   fruit _ _ _ _ _   green _ _ _ _ _

drink _ _ _ _ _   bring _ _ _ _ _   truck _ _ _ _ _

Words with double letters

To practise spelling words with double letters **ee**, and **oo**.

Write **ee** or **oo** to complete the words. Spell each word twice, then cover and try to spell again, on your own this time.

t r _ _   _ _ _ _   _ _ _ _   _ _ _ _

b _ _ t   _ _ _ _   _ _ _ _   _ _ _ _

b _ _   _ _ _   _ _ _   _ _ _

s h _ _ p   _ _ _ _ _   _ _ _ _ _   _ _ _ _ _

d _ _ r   _ _ _ _   _ _ _ _   _ _ _ _

f _ _ t   _ _ _ _   _ _ _ _   _ _ _ _

b _ _ k   _ _ _ _   _ _ _ _   _ _ _ _

m _ _ n   _ _ _ _   _ _ _ _   _ _ _ _

Write **ee** or **oo**.

_ _ k

m _ _

w _ _ f

Spelling

 To practise spelling words with double letters **bb**, **dd**, **ll**, **mm**, **pp**, **rr**, **ss**, and **tt**.

Words with double letters

Choose letters from this list to spell the double letter words:
bb, **dd**, **ll**, **mm**, **pp**, **rr**, **ss**, **tt**. Spell each word twice.

d r e _ _   _ _ _ _ _   _ _ _ _ _

c a _ _ o t  _ _ _ _ _ _   _ _ _ _ _ _

b u _ _ l e   _ _ _ _ _ _   _ _ _ _ _ _

p u _ _ y   _ _ _ _ _   _ _ _ _ _

l e _ _ e r   _ _ _ _ _ _   _ _ _ _ _ _

t e _ _ y   _ _ _ _ _   _ _ _ _ _

w e _ _  _ _ _ _   _ _ _ _

mu _ _ y   _ _ _ _ _   _ _ _ _ _

Underline the double letter words.

Little Tommy Tucker sang for his supper.

Betty Botter bought a bit of better butter.

Words with **qu** and **kn**

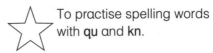

To practise spelling words with **qu** and **kn**.

Practise spelling **qu** words. Write each word twice.

quiet _ _ _ _ _   _ _ _ _ _   quack _ _ _ _ _   _ _ _ _ _

quite _ _ _ _ _   _ _ _ _ _   quiz _ _ _ _   _ _ _ _

quarter _ _ _ _ _ _ _   _ _ _ _ _ _ _

Write **qu** to spell these words. Draw a picture for each one.

_ _ i l t   _ _ e e n

Write **kn** to spell the words. Spell each word twice, then cover and try to spell again, on your own this time.

_ _ e e   _ _ _ _   _ _ _ _   _ _ _ _

_ _ i t   _ _ _ _   _ _ _ _   _ _ _ _

_ _ o t   _ _ _ _   _ _ _ _   _ _ _ _

_ _ i f e   _ _ _ _ _   _ _ _ _ _   _ _ _ _ _

_ _ i g h t   _ _ _ _ _   _ _ _ _ _   _ _ _ _ _

16

Spelling

To practise spelling words with **ph** and **wh**.

Words with **ph** and **wh**

Write **ph** to spell the words. Spell the words twice more.
Match the words to the pictures.

_ _ o t o   _ _ _ _ _   _ _ _ _ _

g r a _ _   _ _ _ _ _   _ _ _ _ _

_ _ o n e   _ _ _ _ _   _ _ _ _ _

Write **wh** to spell the words. Choose and spell each one to
finish the questions.

_ _ o   _ _ a t   _ _ e r e   _ _ e n   _ _ y   _ _ i c h

_ _ _ _ _ _ of these buns do you want?

_ _ _ _ _ is the answer?

_ _ _ _ _ _ are you going to?

_ _ _ is hiding?

_ _ _ do balls bounce?

_ _ _ _ _ is your birthday?

Words with **oa** and **ow**

To practise spelling words
with **oa** and **ow**.

Write **oa** or **ow** to spell the words. Spell each word twice,
then cover and try to spell again, on your own this time.

c _ _ t   _ _ _ _   _ _ _ _   _ _ _ _

b _ _   _ _ _   _ _ _   _ _ _

g _ _ t   _ _ _ _   _ _ _ _   _ _ _ _

c r _ _   _ _ _ _   _ _ _ _   _ _ _ _

s _ _ p   _ _ _ _   _ _ _ _   _ _ _ _

Choose the right words from the list. Spell them.

mow grow flow loaf boat oat float slow cloak

The opposite of fast is _ _ _ _ .

_ _ _ the grass.

The opposite of to sink is to _ _ _ _ _ _ .

Flowers _ _ _ _ in the garden.

Red Riding Hood always wore a red _ _ _ _ _ _ .

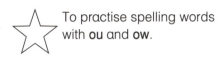

To practise spelling words with **ou** and **ow**.

A word is hidden in each row of the word puzzle.

The picture clues will help you find the words.

Draw a circle around each word. Spell the words you find.

_ _ _ _ _

n	c	l	o	w	n	n	o	c	e
x	s	o	s	h	o	u	t	a	s
p	h	o	u	s	e	n	a	e	t
a	o	u	d	o	w	n	m	x	u
f	r	o	b	d	t	o	w	e	l
b	f	r	o	w	n	g	y	r	c
r	k	l	r	o	u	n	d	t	e

_ _ _ _

_ _ _ _ _

_ _ _ _ _

_ _ _ _ _

Spelling words with **ai**

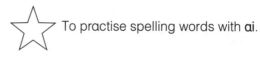

To practise spelling words with ai.

Write **ai** to spell the words. Spell each word twice, then cover the words and try to spell again, on your own this time.

r _ _ n   _ _ _ _   _ _ _ _   _ _ _ _

h _ _ r   _ _ _ _   _ _ _ _   _ _ _ _

p _ _ n t   _ _ _ _ _   _ _ _ _ _   _ _ _ _ _

s n _ _ l   _ _ _ _ _   _ _ _ _ _   _ _ _ _ _

t _ _ l   _ _ _ _   _ _ _ _   _ _ _ _

s t _ _ r s   _ _ _ _ _ _   _ _ _ _ _ _   _ _ _ _ _ _

s _ _ l o r   _ _ _ _ _ _   _ _ _ _ _ _   _ _ _ _ _ _

f _ _ r y   _ _ _ _ _   _ _ _ _ _   _ _ _ _ _

Tick the words that are spelled correctly.

gain ✔   agen   fail   pait   wait   chain

gane   again   faile   pain   wate   chaim

Spelling

 To practise spelling words with different **ea** sounds.

Spelling words with **ea**

Rearrange the letters to spell the words correctly.

Spell each word twice more.

f e a l   _ _ _ _   _ _ _ _   _ _ _ _

s a e   _ _ _   _ _ _   _ _ _

e a d b s   _ _ _ _ _   _ _ _ _ _   _ _ _ _ _

These **ea** words have a different sound.

d e a h   _ _ _ _   _ _ _ _   _ _ _ _

b d r e a   _ _ _ _ _   _ _ _ _ _   _ _ _ _ _

a e p r   _ _ _ _   _ _ _ _   _ _ _ _

Choose **ea** words from the list to finish the story.

leader   east
treasure
heavy   read

One day pirates went looking for _ _ _ _ _ _ _ _ _ . Captain Cutlass was the _ _ _ _ _ _ . He _ _ _ _ his map. "Turn to the _ _ _ _ at the tree," he said. "Now dig!" They found a big box. It was very _ _ _ _ _ _ .

Words that end with **ay**

To practise spelling words with **ay**.

Read the words with **ay**.

| bay | day | hay | lay | pay | ray | say | way |

Do the letter sums to make more words with **ay**.
Spell them twice more.

pl + ay = _ _ _ _   _ _ _ _   _ _ _ _

del + ay = _ _ _ _ _   _ _ _ _ _   _ _ _ _ _

cl + ay = _ _ _ _   _ _ _ _   _ _ _ _

pr + ay = _ _ _ _   _ _ _ _   _ _ _ _

rel + ay = _ _ _ _ _   _ _ _ _ _   _ _ _ _ _

j + ay = _ _ _   _ _ _   _ _ _

Choose one of the new words to finish each sentence.

I ran in the _ _ _ _ _ _ race.

I saw a _ _ _ in the woods.

I made a pot out of _ _ _ _ .

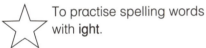

To practise spelling words with ight.

Words that end with **ight**

Spell the words to complete the crossword.
All the words end with **ight**.

I _ _ _ _ _ is the opposite of day.

2 If you can see, you have _ _ _ _ _ _ .

3 The balloon popped. It gave me a _ _ _ _ _ _ _ .

4 Tie the rope. Pull it _ _ _ _ _ _ .

5 What is on TV _ _ _ _ _ _ _ _ ?

6 I have two hands, left and _ _ _ _ _ _ .

Adding **ing**

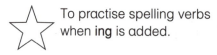

To practise spelling verbs when **ing** is added.

Add **ing** to spell these words. Spell them twice more.

talk + ing = **talking** _ _ _ _ _ _ _   _ _ _ _ _ _ _

sing + ing = _ _ _ _ _ _ _   _ _ _ _ _ _ _   _ _ _ _ _ _ _

read + ing = _ _ _ _ _ _ _ _   _ _ _ _ _ _ _ _   _ _ _ _ _ _ _

For these words you must add an extra letter,
so **I hop** becomes **I am hopping**.

sit + ing = _ _ _ _ _ _ _   _ _ _ _ _ _ _   _ _ _ _ _ _ _

run + ing = _ _ _ _ _ _ _   _ _ _ _ _ _ _   _ _ _ _ _ _ _

skip + ing = _ _ _ _ _ _ _ _   _ _ _ _ _ _ _ _   _ _ _ _ _ _ _ _

In words that end in **e**, the **e** is left out when **ing** is added.
For example **I hope** becomes **I am hoping**.

make + ing = _ _ _ _ _ _ _

share + ing = _ _ _ _ _ _ _ _

dance + ing = _ _ _ _ _ _ _ _

bite + ing = _ _ _ _ _ _ _

write + ing = _ _ _ _ _ _ _ _

To practise spelling verbs
when **ing** is added.

Add **ing** to these words. Spell them twice more.

win 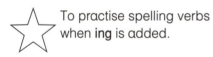 _____   _____

hum _____   _____   _____

cut _____   _____   _____

get _____   _____   _____

slip _____   _____   _____

swim _____   _____   _____

take _____   _____   _____

come _____   _____   _____

smile _____   _____   _____

give _____   _____   _____

wave _____   _____   _____

use _____   _____   _____

Adding **s**

Read the singular words. Spell the plural word for each one.
Some plurals are spelled by adding **s**, and some by adding **es**.

plurals with **s**	plurals with **es**

plurals with **s**

bell _ _ _ _ _

girl _ _ _ _ _

toy _ _ _ _

mug _ _ _ _

paint _ _ _ _ _ _

apple _ _ _ _ _ _

bear _ _ _ _ _

robot _ _ _ _ _ _

plate _ _ _ _ _ _

chair _ _ _ _ _ _

rabbit _ _ _ _ _ _ _

plurals with **es**

fish _ _ _ _ _ _

dress _ _ _ _ _ _ _

dish _ _ _ _ _ _

watch _ _ _ _ _ _ _

witch _ _ _ _ _ _ _

wish _ _ _ _ _ _

bench _ _ _ _ _ _ _

potato _ _ _ _ _ _ _ _

cross _ _ _ _ _ _ _

tomato _ _ _ _ _ _ _ _

church _ _ _ _ _ _ _ _

Spelling

 To practise spelling plurals ending **ies**, and plurals that do not follow rules.

Spell the plural for the words ending in **y**.

Add **s** for these words	These words lose the **y** and have **ies** added
day days	baby _ _ _ _ _ _
play _ _ _ _ _ _	pony _ _ _ _ _ _
bay _ _ _ _ _	daisy _ _ _ _ _ _ _
boy _ _ _ _ _	story _ _ _ _ _ _ _

The plurals for these words do not follow rules.
Tick the correct spelling and spell it twice.

mouse   mouses   mice   _ _ _ _   _ _ _ _

leaf   leafs   leaves   _ _ _ _ _ _   _ _ _ _ _ _

woman   women   womans   _ _ _ _ _   _ _ _ _ _

sheep   sheeps   sheap   _ _ _ _ _   _ _ _ _ _

man   men   mans   _ _ _   _ _ _

foot   foots   feet   _ _ _ _   _ _ _ _

27

Words that rhyme

 To recognise rhyming words with common letter patterns.

Words that rhyme often have the same letter endings, as in **pan** and **fan**, **sell** and **tell**.
Find a word that rhymes with each of the words below.
Choose from the words in the box. Spell it.

wing   *sing*

sack   _ _ _ _

cake   _ _ _ _

hand   _ _ _ _

well   _ _ _ _

kick   _ _ _ _

lend   _ _ _ _

hill   _ _ _ _

gold   _ _ _ _

ball   _ _ _ _

fair   _ _ _ _

pick

hold

band

send

pair

make

wall

sing

bill

bell

back

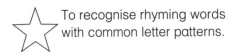
To recognise rhyming words with common letter patterns.

Words that rhyme

Read the poems and underline the words that rhyme.
Spell the words in the rhyme boxes.

Hey, diddle diddle,
The cat and the fiddle,
The cow jumped
    over the moon.
The little dog laughed
    to see such fun,
And the dish ran away
    with the spoon.

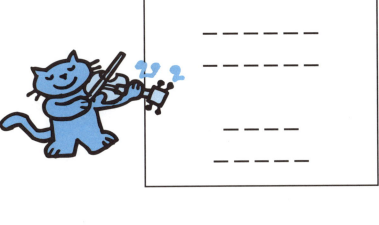

_ _ _ _ _ _

_ _ _ _ _ _

_ _ _ _

_ _ _ _ _

Ding dong bell,
Pussy's in the well!
Who put her in?
Little Tommy Thin.
Who pulled her out?
Little Johnny Stout.

_ _ _ _

_ _ _ _

_ _

_ _ _ _

_ _ _

_ _ _ _ _

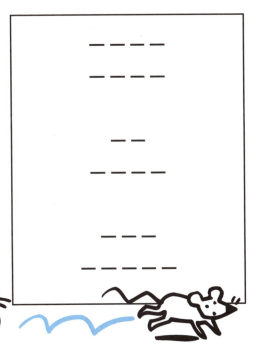

Spelling

Number words

To practise spelling number words one to twenty.

Cover the words and try to spell them on your own.

1 one _ _ _	11 eleven _ _ _ _ _ _
2 two _ _ _	12 twelve _ _ _ _ _ _
3 three _ _ _ _ _	13 thirteen _ _ _ _ _ _ _ _
4 four _ _ _ _	14 fourteen _ _ _ _ _ _ _ _
5 five _ _ _ _	15 fifteen _ _ _ _ _ _ _
6 six _ _ _	16 sixteen _ _ _ _ _ _ _
7 seven _ _ _ _ _	17 seventeen _ _ _ _ _ _ _ _ _
8 eight _ _ _ _ _	18 eighteen _ _ _ _ _ _ _ _
9 nine _ _ _ _	19 nineteen _ _ _ _ _ _ _ _
10 ten _ _ _	20 twenty _ _ _ _ _ _

Spelling

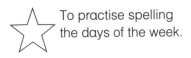

To practise spelling
the days of the week.

Days of the week

Rearrange the letters to spell the days of the week.

daySun _Sunday_

ridayF _ _ _ _ _ _

Mandoy _ _ _ _ _ _

Sutarday _ _ _ _ _ _ _ _

yasdueT _ _ _ _ _ _ _

Wendesday _ _ _ _ _ _ _ _ _

Thrusday _ _ _ _ _ _ _ _

Spelling

Months of the year

Tick the correct spellings of the months of the year and spell them again.

January ✓   Janury   _January_

February   Febuary   _ _ _ _ _ _ _ _

March   March   _ _ _ _ _

Aprul   April   _ _ _ _ _

May   Mae   _ _ _

Juin   June   _ _ _ _

July   Julie   _ _ _ _

Augast   August   _ _ _ _ _ _

Septembur   September   _ _ _ _ _ _ _ _ _

October   Octobur   _ _ _ _ _ _ _

November   Novumber   _ _ _ _ _ _ _ _

December   Decenbur   _ _ _ _ _ _ _ _